Smithsonian

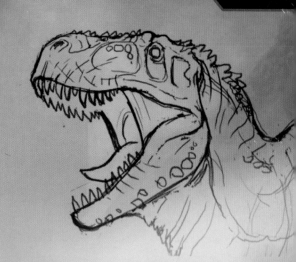

HOW TO DRAW
INCREDIBLE
DINOSAURS

WRITTEN BY KRISTEN MCCURRY
ILLUSTRATED BY JUAN CALLE

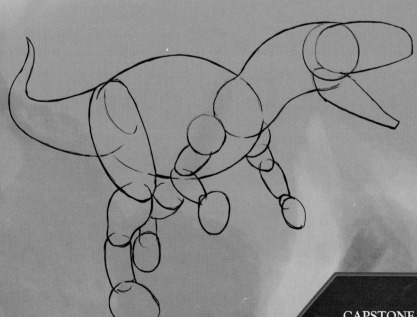

CAPSTONE PRESS
a capstone imprint

TABLE OF CONTENTS

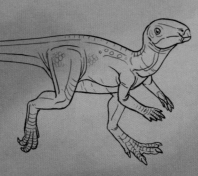

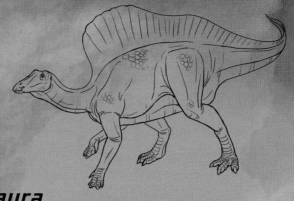

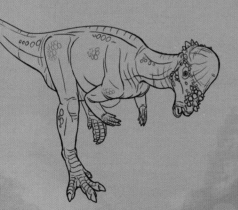

DINOSAUR ERA

TRIASSIC PERIOD

251 MILLION YEARS AGO

JURASSIC PERIOD

199 MILLION YEARS AGO

CRETACEOUS PERIOD

145 to 65 MILLION YEARS AGO

STEP 1

STEP 2

STEP 3

Albertosaurus looked similar to its cousin, Tyrannosaurus, but its powerful body was smaller. Albertosaurus was a meat-eater and used its curved, serrated teeth to tear into flesh and bone. It chased live prey but would also eat dead animals it found.

STEP 4

STEP 5

STEP 1

STEP 2

STEP 3

Allosaurus used its strong back legs to run across the plains after prey. It chased herds of plant-eating animals, singling out a member to kill. Allosaurus had long arms that ended in three claws. Above each eye it had a narrow, raised ridge, which may have been brightly colored to attract mates.

STEP 4

STEP 5

ANKYLOSAURUS
Cretaceous Period

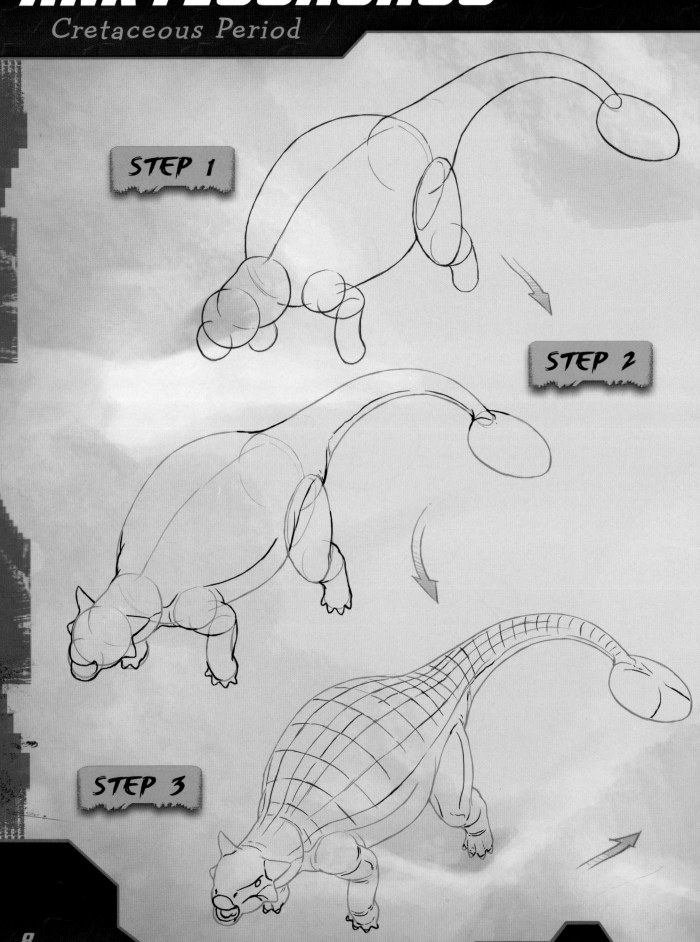

STEP 1

STEP 2

STEP 3

Ankylosaurus was a plant-eater built like a tank. It had a covering of armor over its head, body, and tail. Even its eyes had eyelids of bone. Most of the armor was made up of flat bony plates with spikes sticking up. Ankylosaurus' best defense may have been its strong, clubbed tail, which it could swing like a wrecking ball.

STEP 4

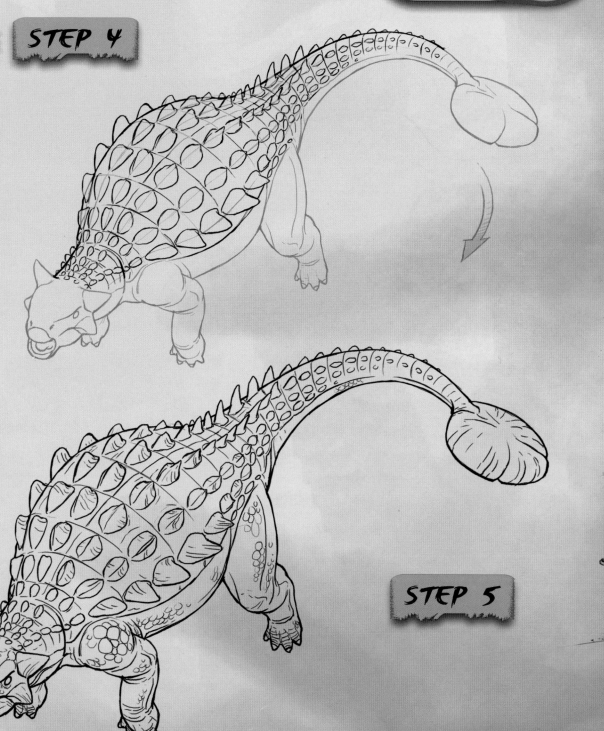

STEP 5

BRACHIOSAURUS
Jurassic Period

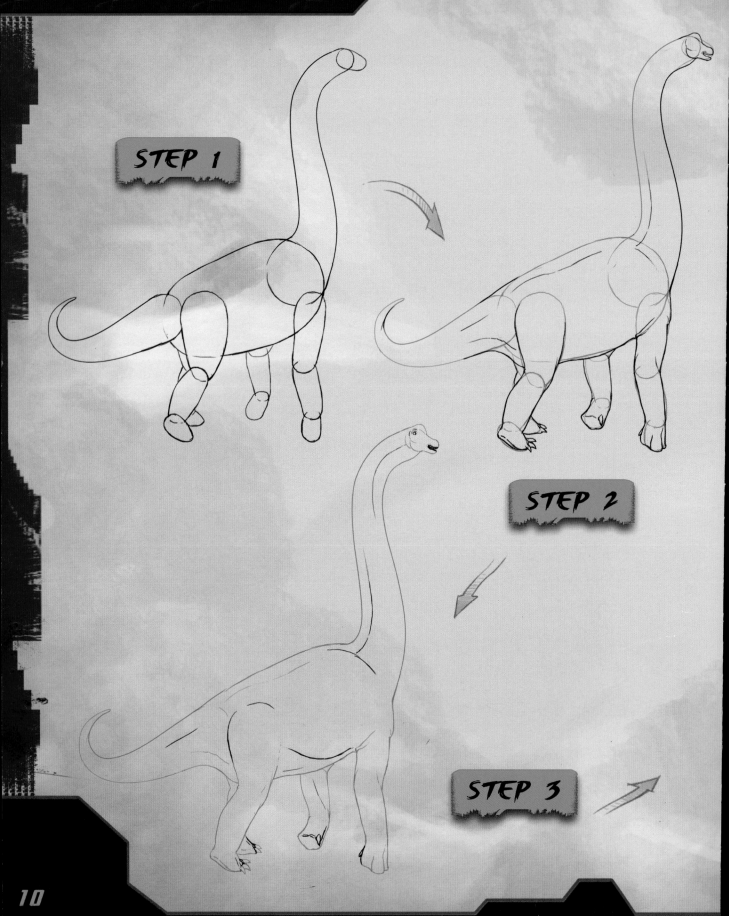

STEP 1

STEP 2

STEP 3

Brachiosaurus was a massive dinosaur that weighed as much as six elephants. Its incredible height allowed it to eat plants that few other creatures could reach. To feed its large body, Brachiosaurus may have needed to eat for more than half of the day.

STEP 4

STEP 5

CHUNGKINGOSAURUS
Jurassic Period

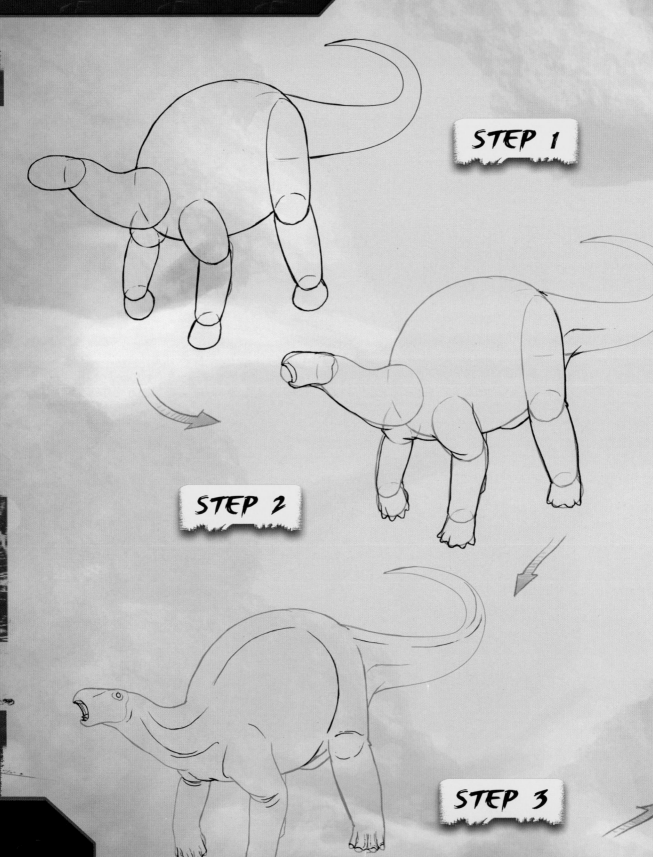

STEP 1

STEP 2

STEP 3

Chungkingosaurus was a type of small stegosaur found in China. This plant-eater had a small head and a double row of spikelike plates running down its back. Scientists believe Chungkingosaurus may have had five sharp spikes at the end of its tail. Other stegosaurs had only four.

STEP 4

STEP 5

COELOPHYSIS
Triassic Period

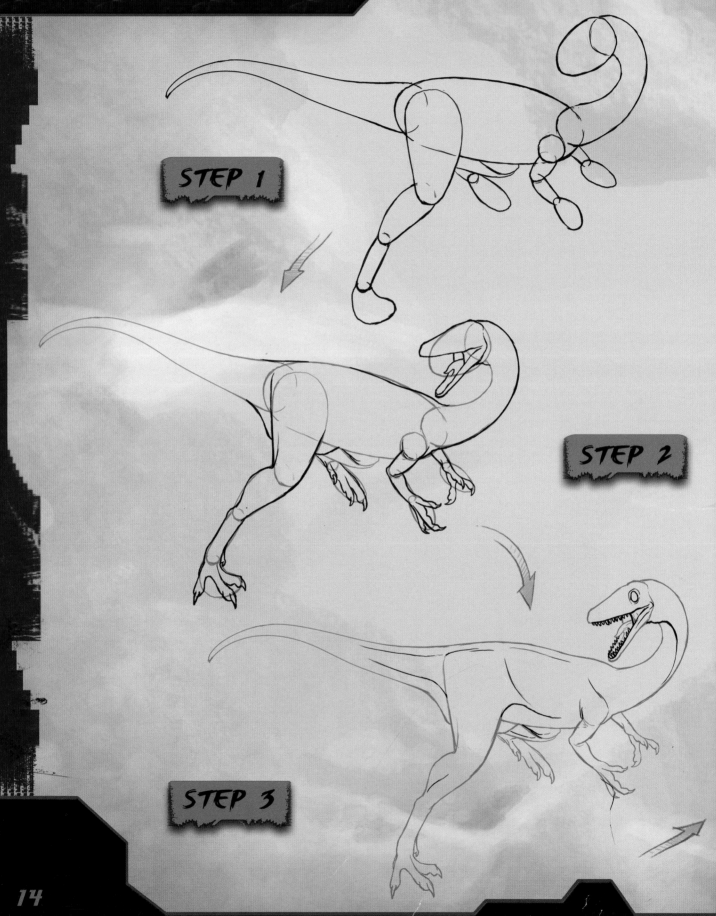

STEP 1

STEP 2

STEP 3

Coelophysis was one of the first meat-eating dinosaurs. This small, lightweight hunter traveled in a pack and likely fed on small reptiles and other creatures. Coelophysis was a fast and active predator. It had large eyes and serrated teeth for finding and eating prey.

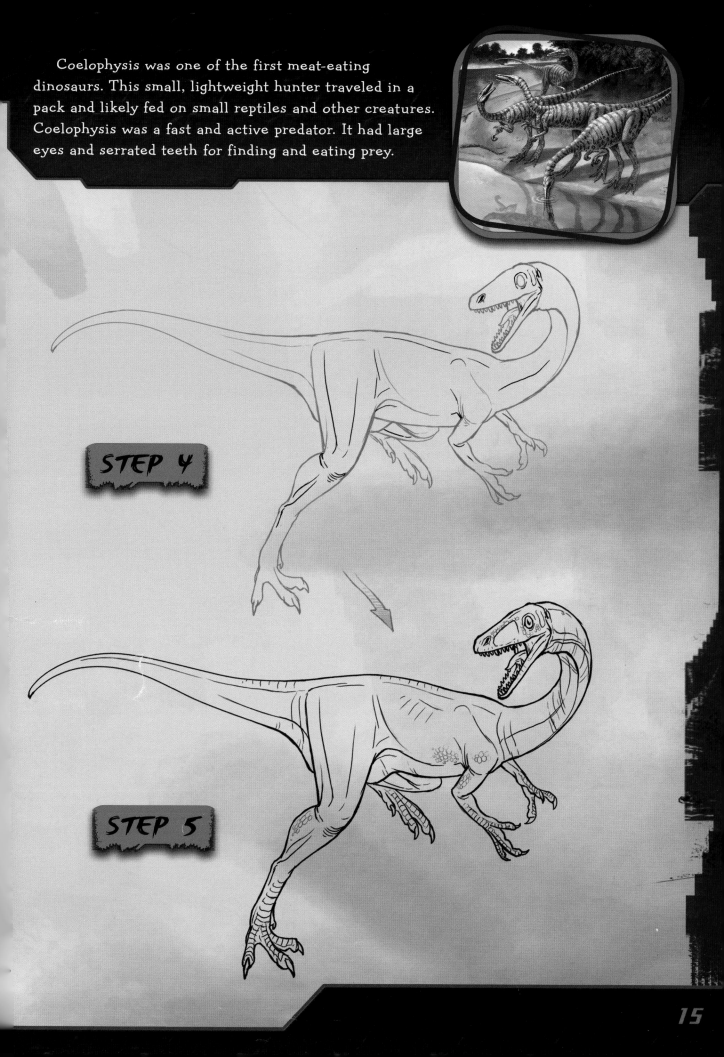

STEP 4

STEP 5

CORYTHOSAURUS

Cretaceous Period

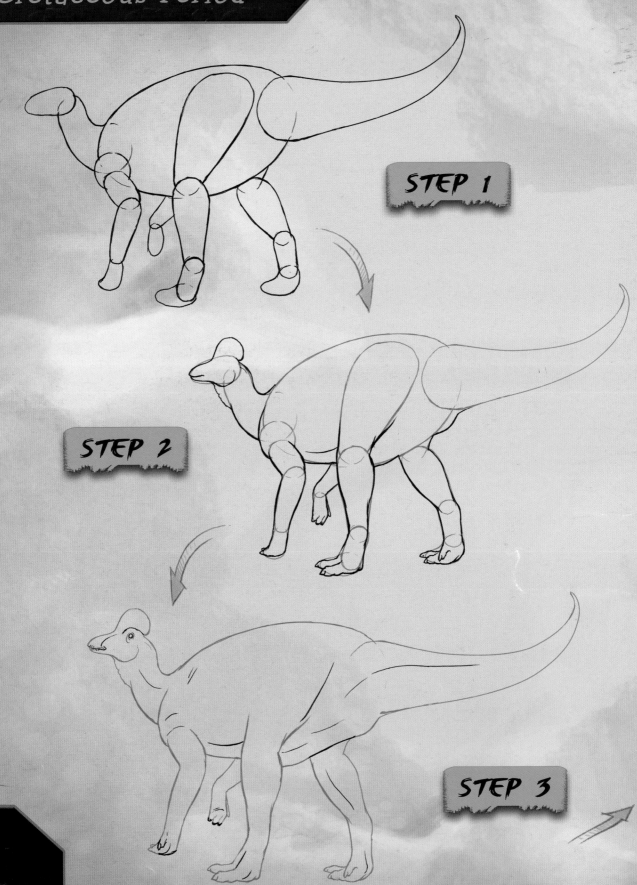

STEP 1

STEP 2

STEP 3

Corythosaurus was a duck-billed plant-eater with a large rounded crest on its head. Scientists believe this crest held a hollow chamber that helped the dinosaur make loud sounds. Corythosaurus had padded hands and short front legs. It walked on all fours but ran on its hind legs.

STEP 4

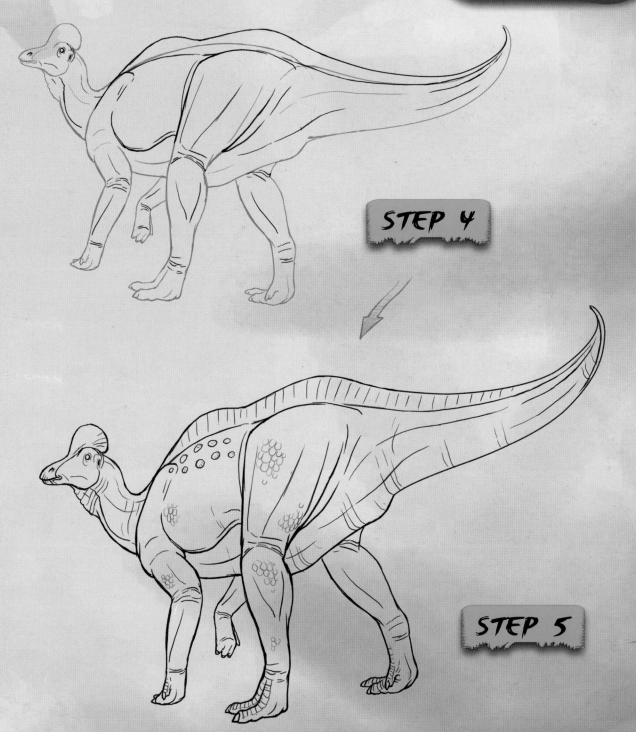

STEP 5

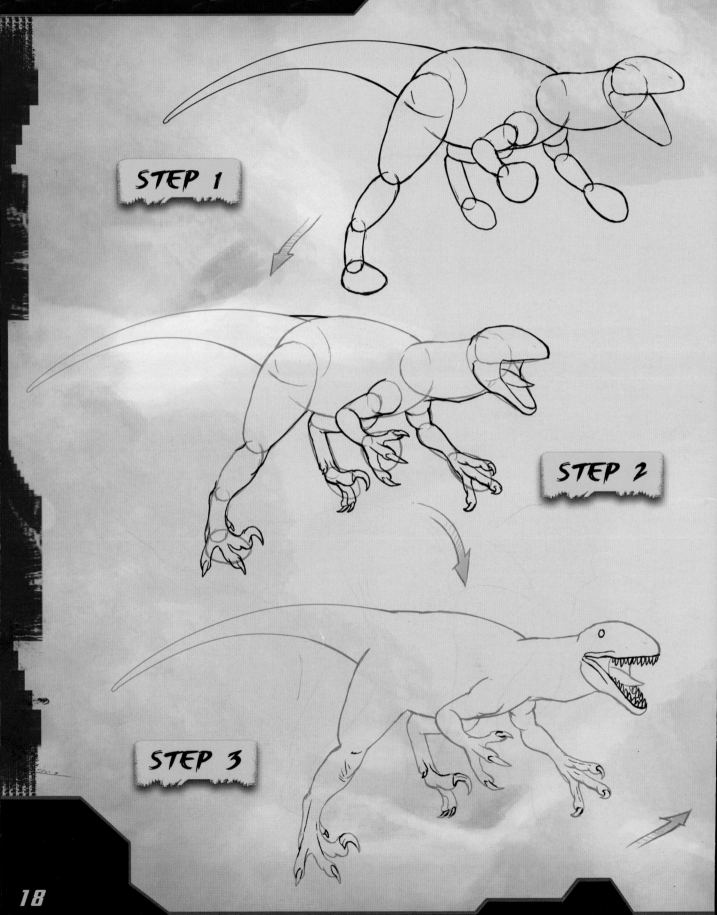

STEP 1

STEP 2

STEP 3

Deinonychus was a fierce pack hunter. It had a large talon on the second toe of each foot that it used to tear meat. In fact, the name Deinonychus means "terrible claw." These small but deadly dinosaurs had relatively large brains and strong eyesight. They preyed on dinosaurs much bigger than themselves.

STEP 4

STEP 5

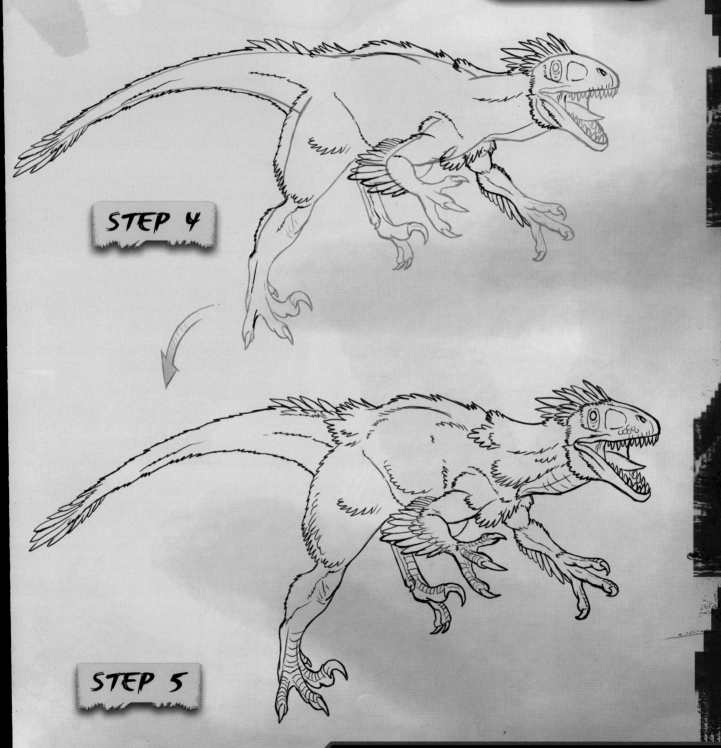

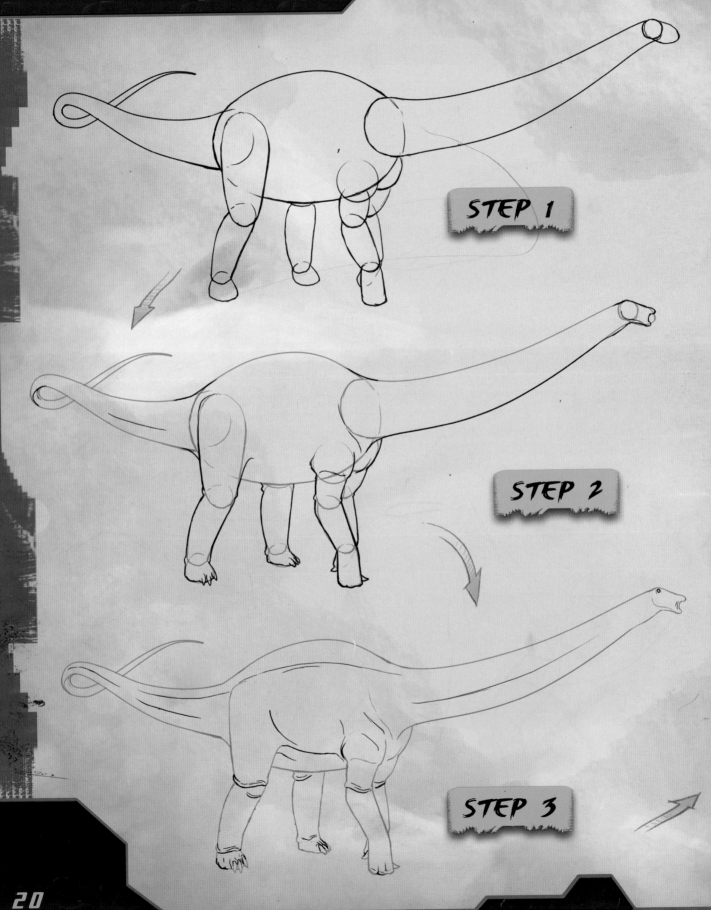

STEP 1

STEP 2

STEP 3

At nearly 90 feet (27 meters) long, Diplodocus was one of the longest land animals in history. Though its neck was very long, Diplodocus moved its head from side to side, eating from plants near the ground or just above its shoulder height.

STEP 4

STEP 5

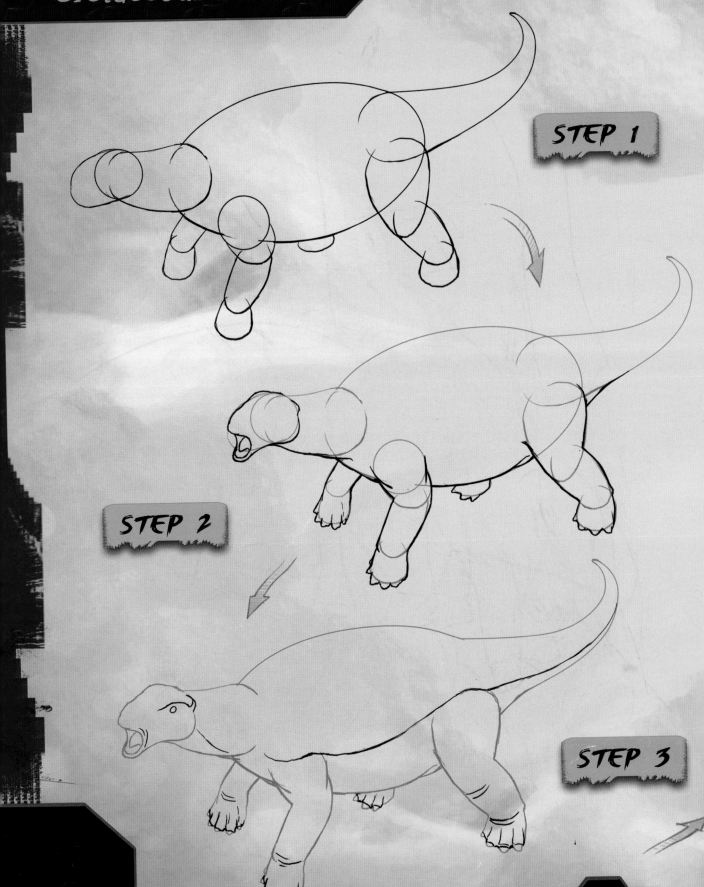

STEP 1

STEP 2

STEP 3

Edmontonia was a short-legged dinosaur with armor on its back and spikes coming out its sides. These features helped protect it from the huge meat-eating Gorgosaurus and other predators. Edmontonia had a beak that helped it gather plants to eat. Some scientists believe Edmontonia could make honking sounds.

STEP 4

STEP 5

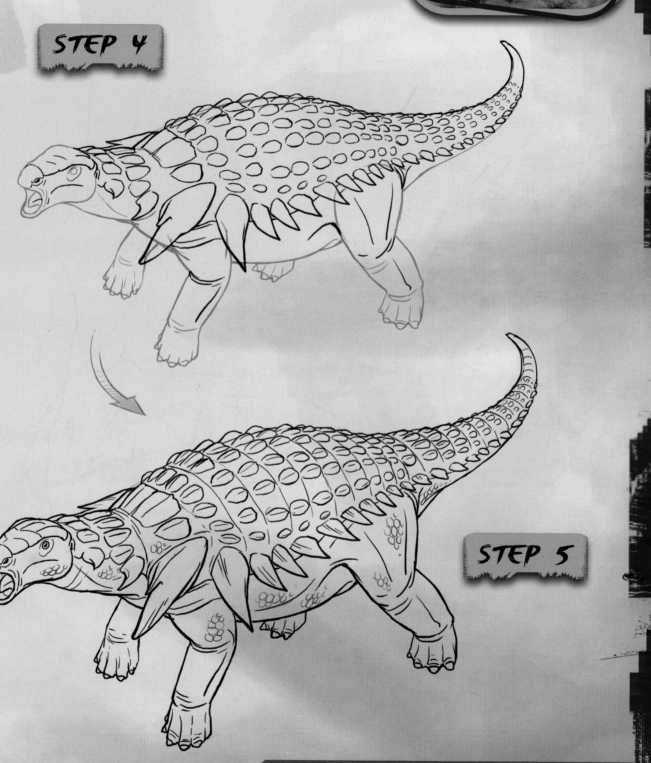

STEP 1

STEP 2

STEP 3

Edmontosaurus could crunch through tough trees and plants with its strong jaw and more than 700 teeth. This dinosaur spent most of its time on land. T. rex was one of its predators, but Edmontosaurus was able to remain safe if it stayed in a herd.

STEP 4

STEP 5

STEP 1

STEP 2

STEP 3

Falcarius, one of the raptor dinosaurs, ate both plants and meat. It used its hands to reach for plants and had long, curved claws to strip leaves from their branches. Falcarius had leaf-shaped teeth. It walked on two legs and had a featherlike coating.

STEP 4

STEP 5

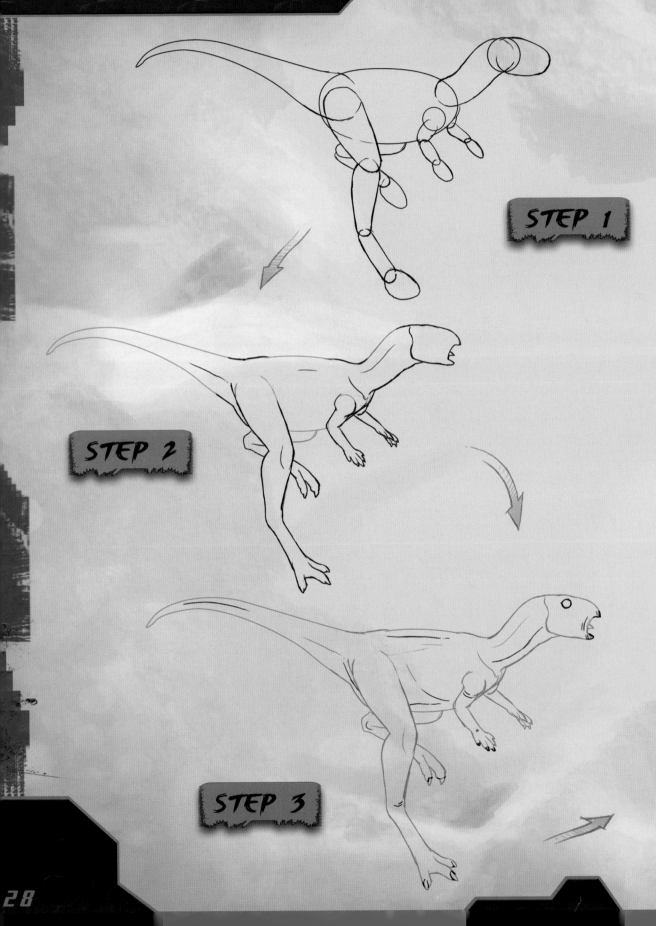

STEP 1

STEP 2

STEP 3

Gasparinisaura was a small dinosaur that may have lived in herds to help protect itself from larger predators. It walked on its powerful hind legs and had very short arms.

STEP 4

STEP 5

GASTONIA
Cretaceous Period

STEP 1

STEP 2

STEP 3

Gastonia was an armored, spiky plant-eater. This dinosaur used its long, sharp spikes for defense against its many predators. Gastonia's short height and stumpy legs made it a slow mover. But these features also helped protect Gastonia's soft underbelly from predators' teeth.

STEP 4

STEP 5

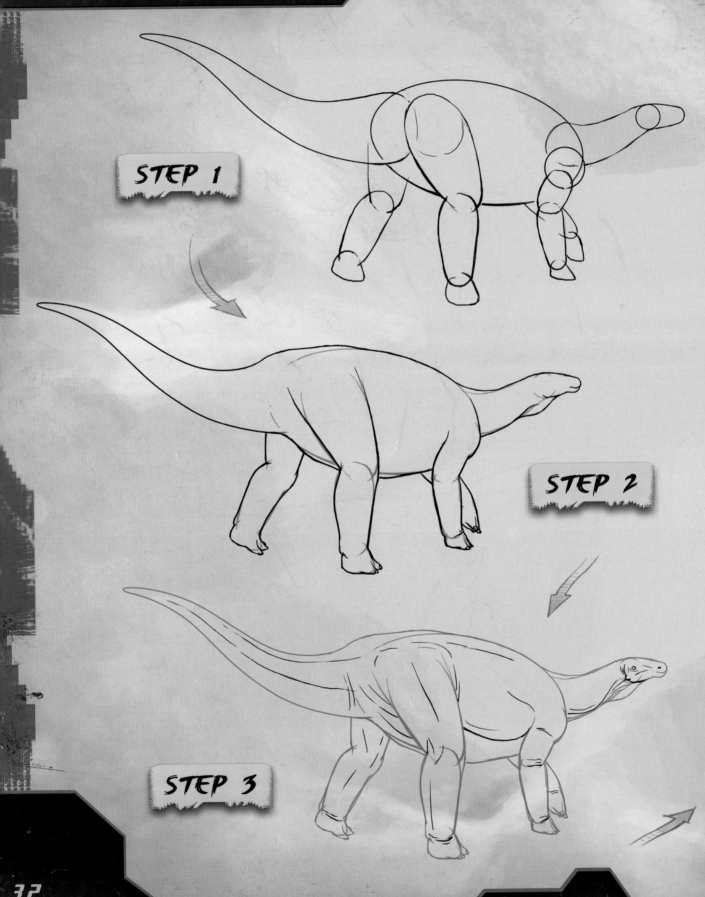

STEP 1

STEP 2

STEP 3

Gigantspinosaurus was a large spiked dinosaur in the stegosaur group. In fact, its name means "giant spined lizard." Two long spikes jutted out from its shoulder blades. This plant-eater had a small head and was about 13 feet (4 meters) long.

STEP 4

STEP 5

KENTROSAURUS

Jurassic Period

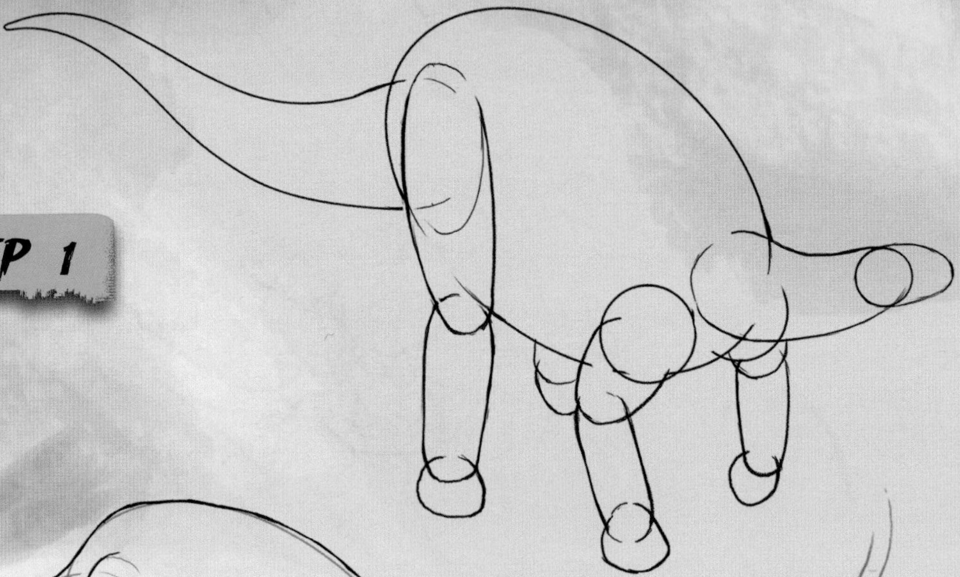

STEP 1

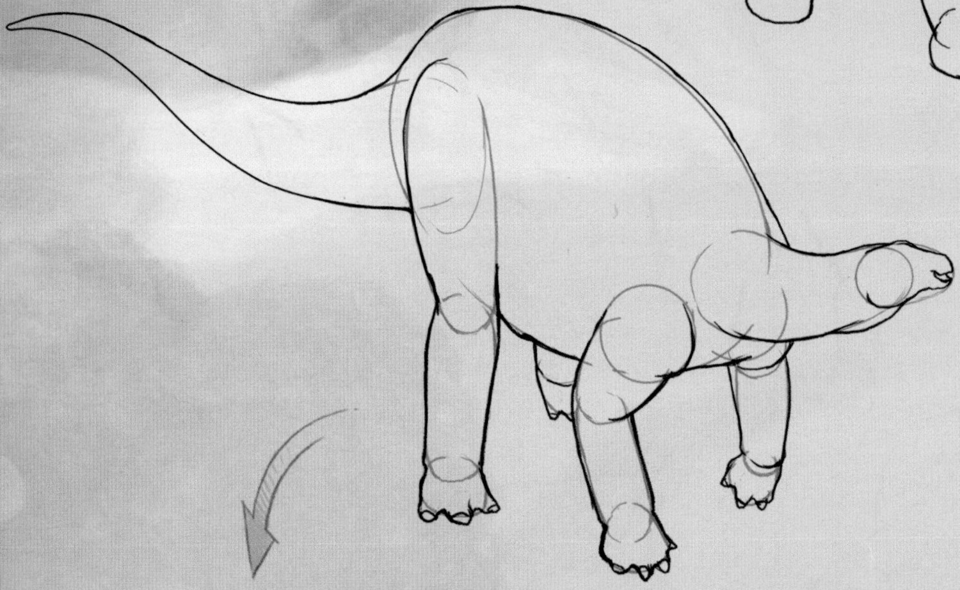

STEP 2

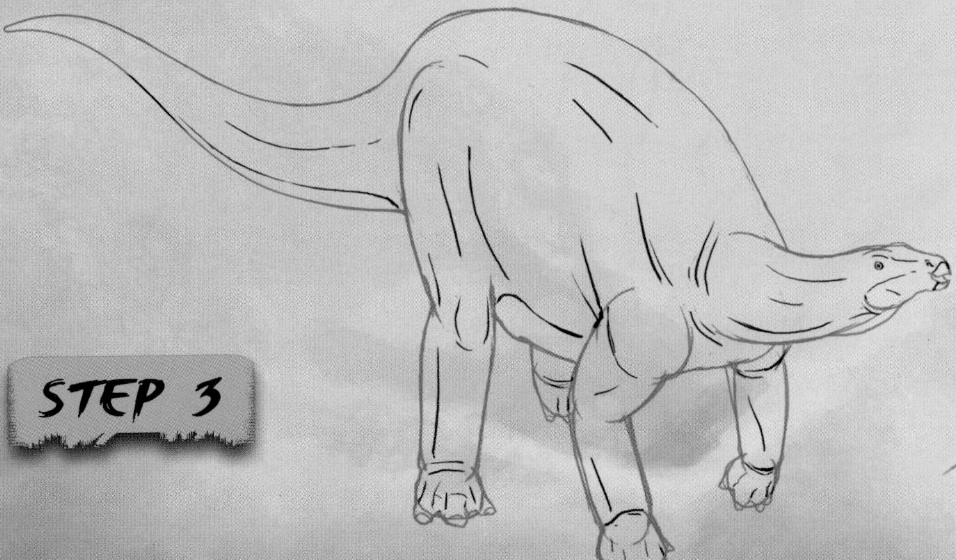

STEP 3

This small stegosaur had large bony plates that ran down its back in pairs and two long spikes over its shoulders. Blood running through the plates on its back helped warm or cool the dinosaur as needed. Kentrosaurus was a plant-eater and was probably hunted by allosaurs.

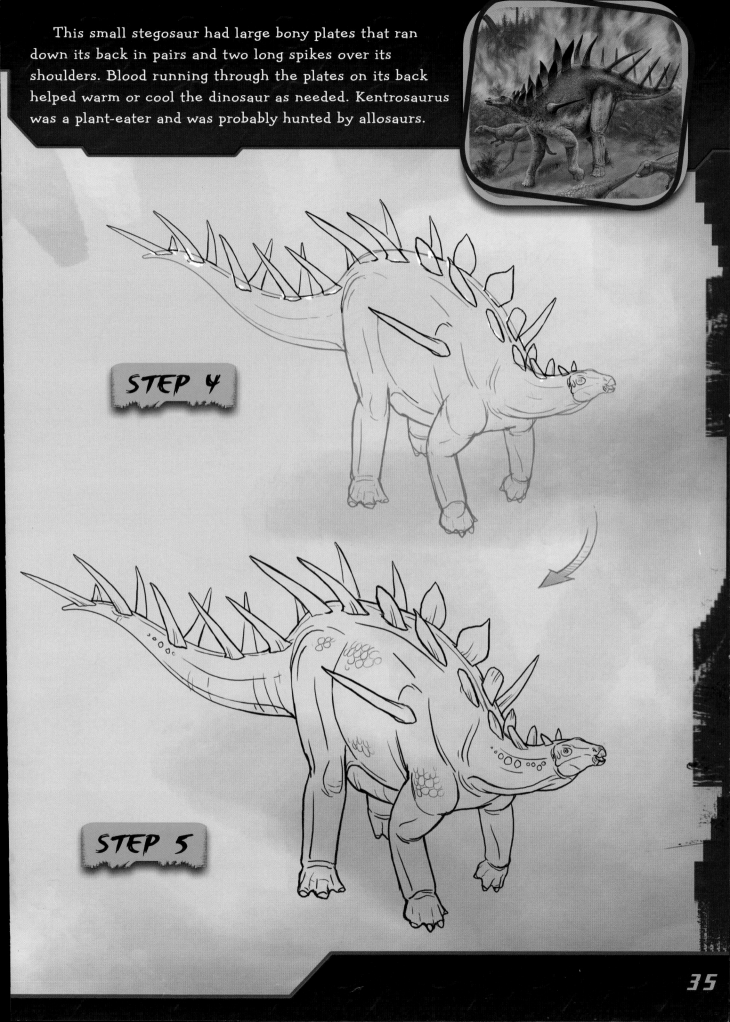

STEP 4

STEP 5

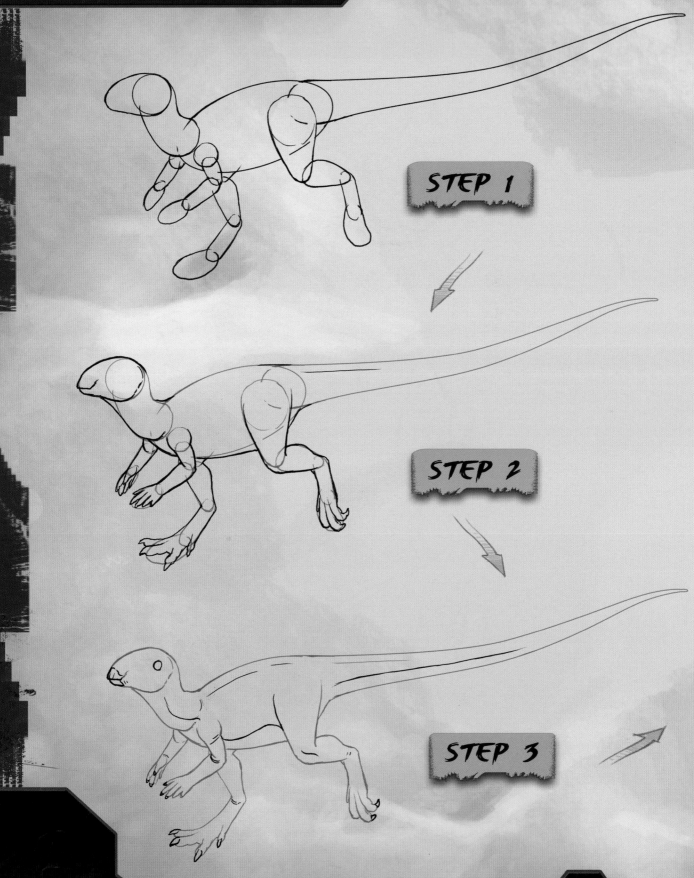

STEP 1

STEP 2

STEP 3

Leaellynasaura was a small plant-eater that lived in southern Australia. It may have been warm-blooded to help it survive in the cold. Leaellynasaura had a large brain, which shows that it was intelligent. It also had large eyes that may have helped it to see in the dark winter months.

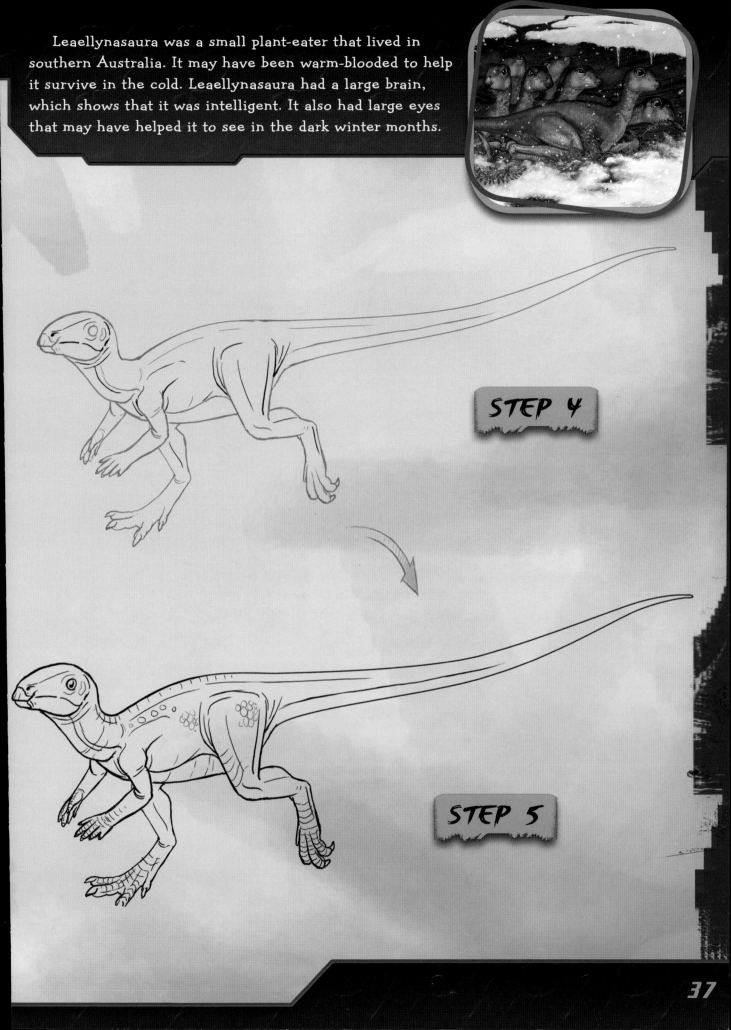

STEP 4

STEP 5

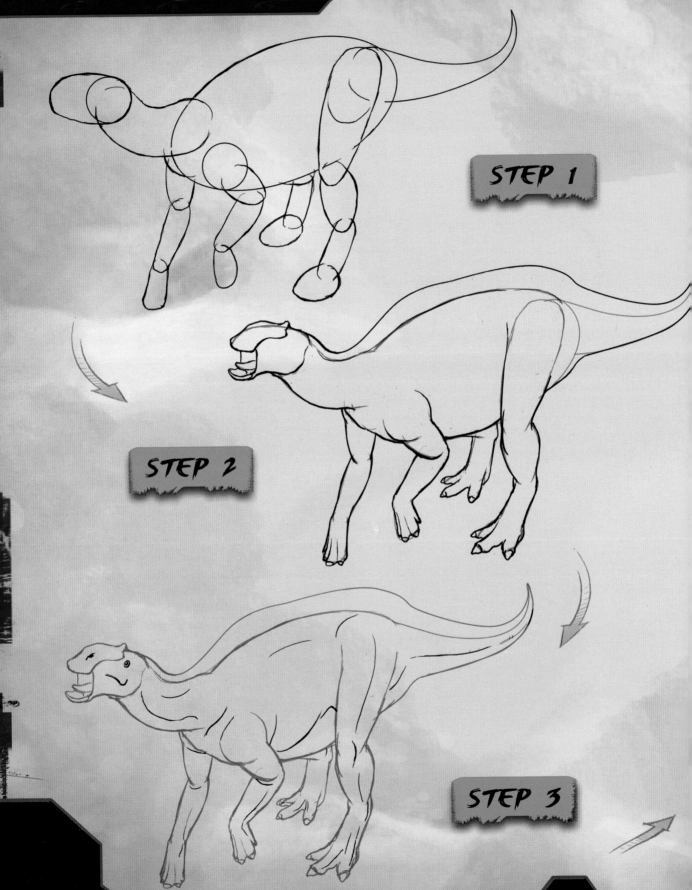

STEP 1

STEP 2

STEP 3

Maiasaura means "good mother lizard." Scientists gave the duck-billed dinosaur its name because they believe it cared for its young after the eggs hatched. Maiasaura was 30 feet (9 meters) long and ate plants constantly to feed its large body.

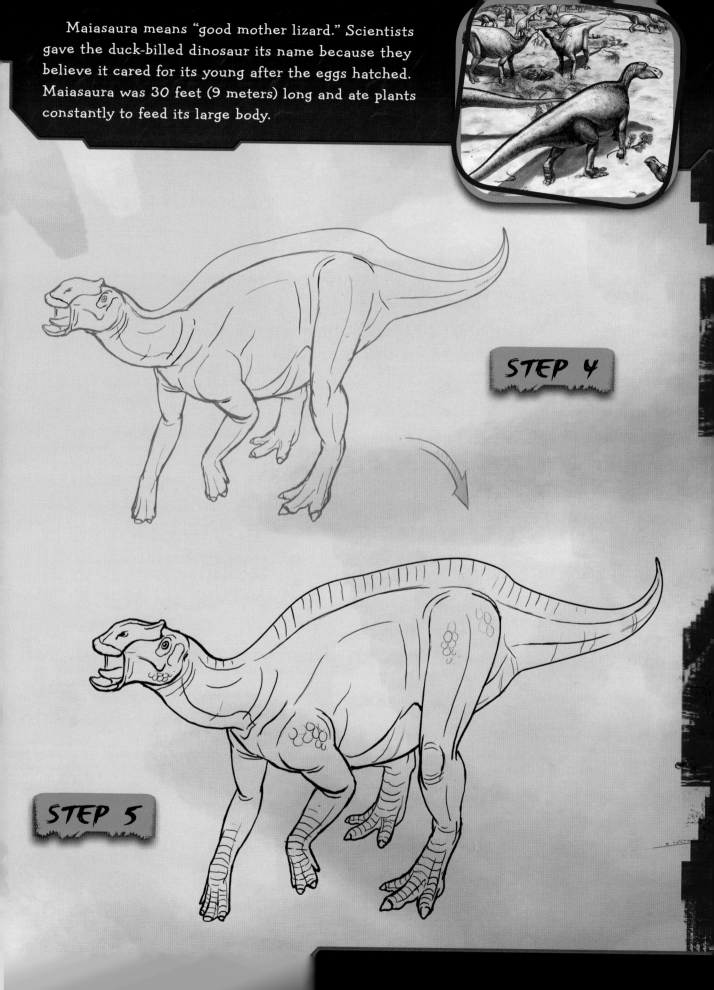

STEP 4

STEP 5

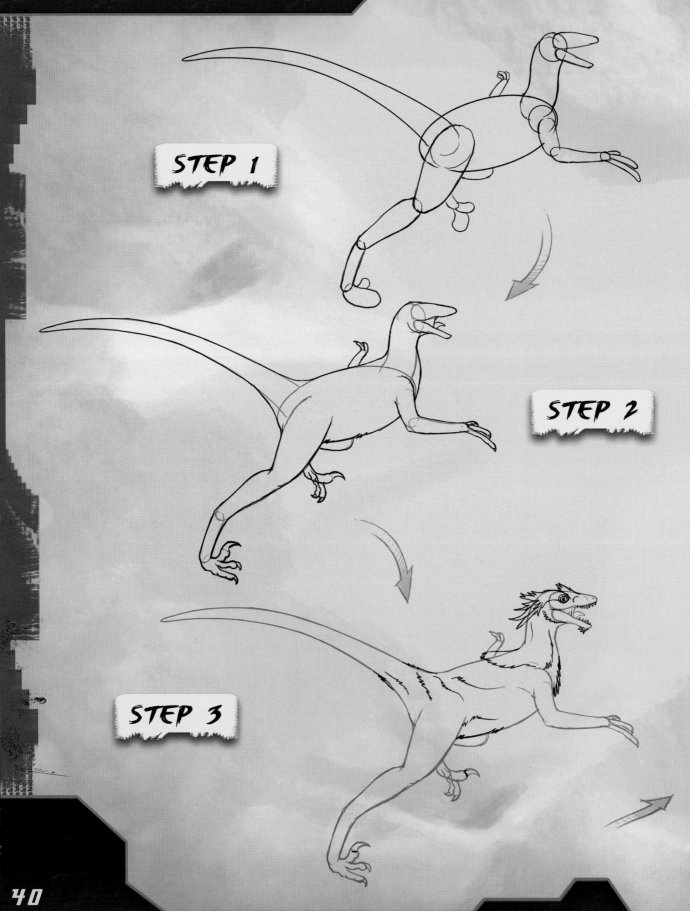

STEP 1

STEP 2

STEP 3

Microraptor was a tiny, feathered dinosaur that weighed only 3 to 4 pounds (1.4 to 1.8 kilograms). It had wings on both its arms and legs and was able to glide from tree to tree. Its feathers may have helped keep it warm. Microraptor was a meat-eater. It used a claw on its middle toe for defense.

STEP 4

STEP 5

OMEISAURUS
Jurassic Period

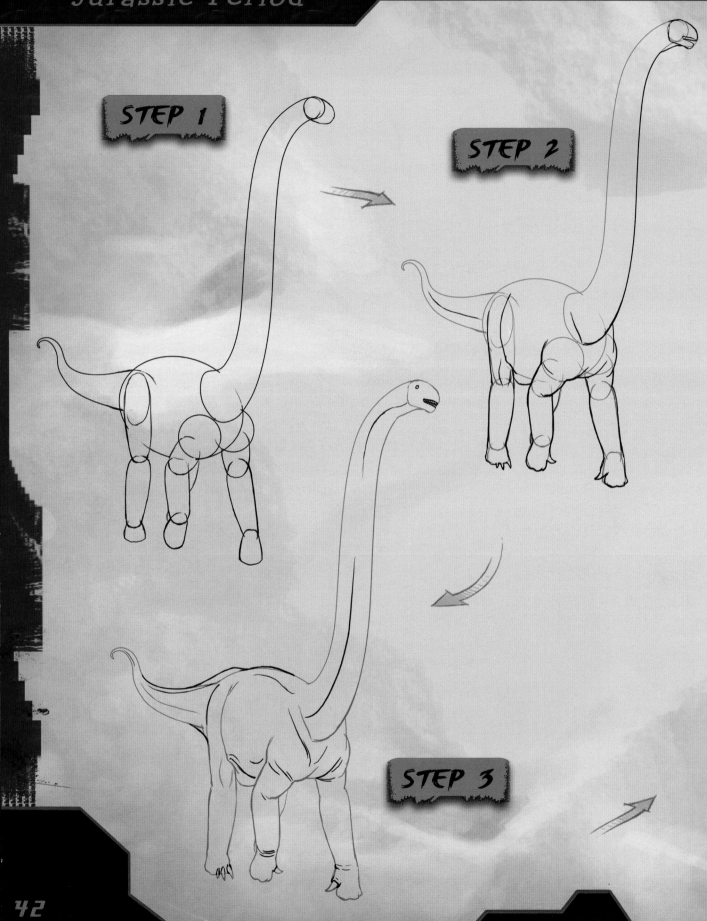

STEP 1

STEP 2

STEP 3

Omeisaurus had one of the longest necks of all the long-necked dinosaurs. Its spoon-shaped teeth helped it eat plants. The adult Omeisaurus probably had few predators because of its incredible size.

STEP 4

STEP 5

STEP 1

STEP 2

STEP 3

Ouranosaurus had an unusual skeleton. This plant-eater had a large head with long jaws. It may have had a horny beak on the front of its long snout. Ouranosaurus also had a large sail on its back, which may have helped it to stay cool in its desert home.

STEP 4

STEP 5

PACHYCEPHALOSAURUS

Cretaceous Period

STEP 1

STEP 2

STEP 3

Plant-eater Pachycephalosaurus was the largest of the "thick-headed dinosaurs." Its domed head was smooth and round, and the top of its skull could be 9 inches (23 centimeters) thick. It may have engaged in head-butting with other males of its kind.

STEP 4

STEP 5

STEP 1

STEP 2

STEP 3

This dinosaur was one of the largest of its time period. Plateosaurus was likely able to walk on either two or four legs. It used its long neck and great height to feed off high tree branches. Plateosaurus may have used its clawed thumbs for defense.

STEP 4

STEP 5

STEP 1

STEP 2

STEP 3

Rugops means "wrinkle face." This wrinkly faced dinosaur was a meat-eater with a rounded snout and small teeth. It likely ate animals that were already dead as well as hunted live ones. Rugops had two rows of seven holes on its skull. Scientists believe they may have been from a fleshy crest on the dinosaur's face.

STEP 4

STEP 5

STEGOSAURUS
Jurassic Period

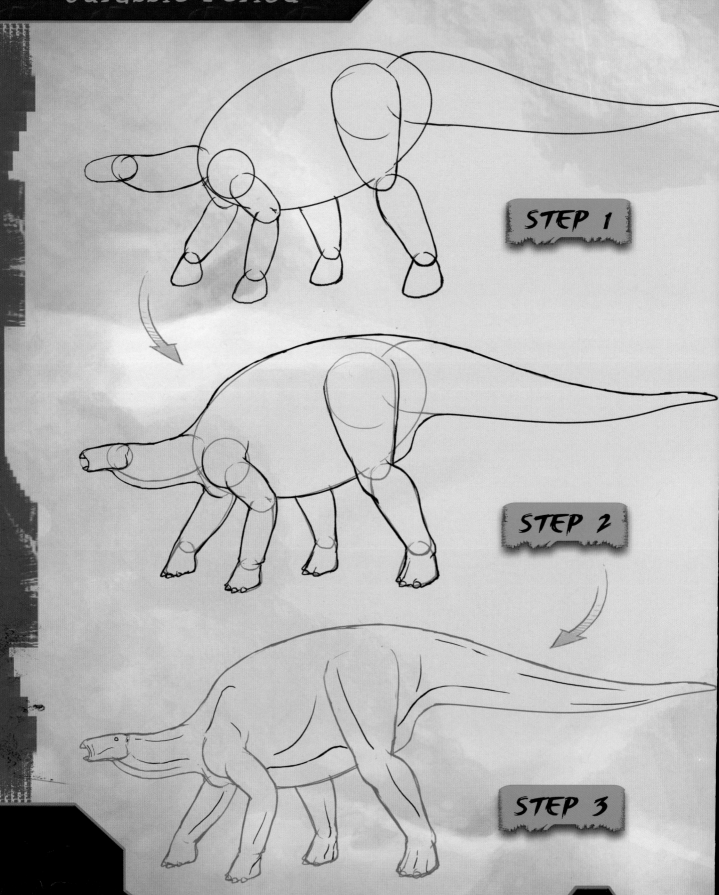

STEP 1

STEP 2

STEP 3

Stegosaurus had two rows of large bony plates running down its back. At the end of its tail it had two pairs of spikes. These spikes may have been for defense. Stegosaurus had a small brain, but good armor. Armored bumps in the skin under its neck may have protected this plant-eater from predators.

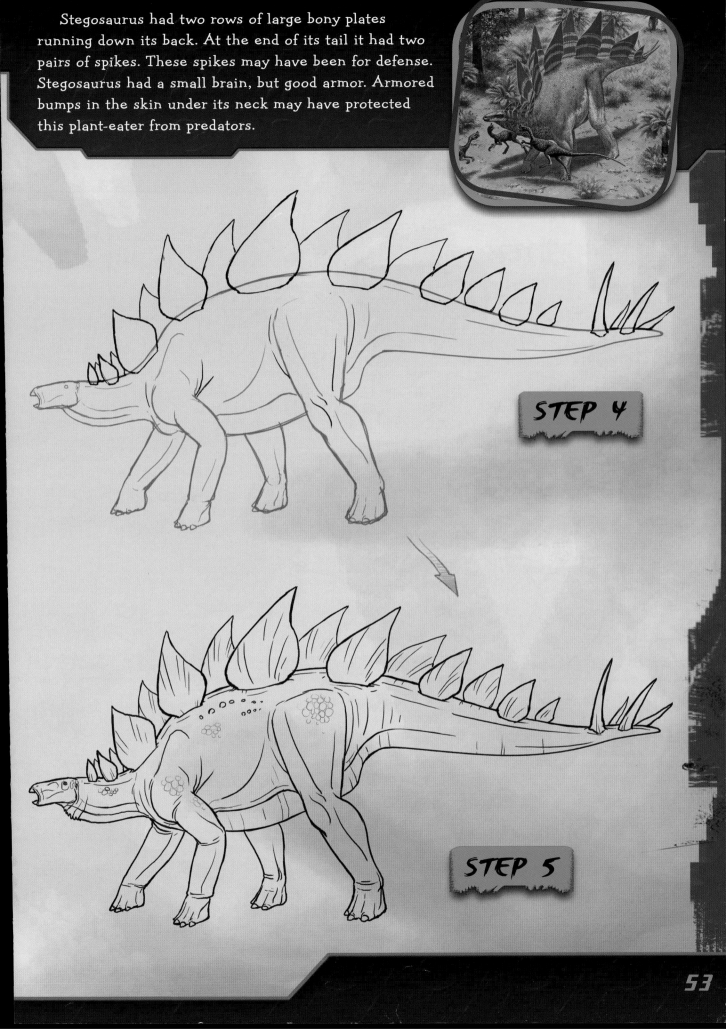

STEP 4

STEP 5

STEP 1

STEP 2

STEP 3

Styracosaurus had an unusual spiked frill at the back of its head. It also had a long horn at the top of its nose like a rhinoceros. These spikes and horn likely served as both defense tools and to attract mates. Styracosaurus was a herd dinosaur with jaws built to chop up the plants it ate.

STEP 4

STEP 5

Cretaceous Period

STEP 1

STEP 2

STEP 3

Thescelosaurus stood on stocky hind legs and was likely a swift runner. It had no teeth at the front of its jaws. Thescelosaurus may have had coloring that helped it blend in with its surroundings to avoid predators.

STEP 4

STEP 5

TRICERATOPS
Cretaceous Period

STEP 1

STEP 2

STEP 3

Triceratops was the biggest of the horned dinosaurs. It had three horns and a giant frill at the back of its head. It may have used its horns in battles against other triceratops. This giant plant-eater weighed 6 to 8 tons (5.4 to 7.3 metric tons).

STEP 4

STEP 5

TYRANNOSAURUS
Cretaceous Period

STEP 1

STEP 2

STEP 3

Tyrannosaurus was one of the fiercest meat-eaters to have roamed the earth. Its big teeth could slice through meat and bone. Tyrannosaurus would hunt and kill prey or eat dead animals it found. Scientists believe it could eat up to 100 pounds (45 kilograms) of meat in a single bite.

STEP 4

STEP 5

VELOCIRAPTOR
Cretaceous Period

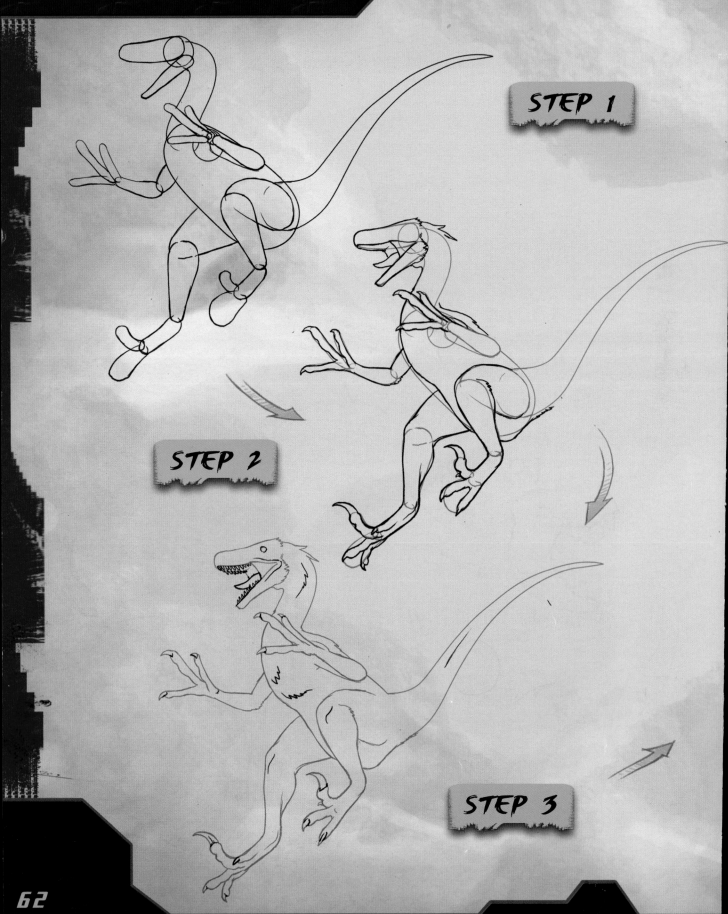

STEP 1

STEP 2

STEP 3

Velociraptor was small, fast, feathered, and fierce. It had sharp, jagged teeth and a deadly claw on each hand, which it used to rip into prey. Velociraptor's long tail helped it keep its balance while attacking or fighting.

STEP 4

STEP 5

Capstone Press
1710 Roe Crest Drive
North Mankato, Minnesota 56003
www.capstonepub.com

Library of Congress Cataloging-in-Publication Data
McCurry, Kristen.
   How to draw incredible dinosaurs / by Kristen McCurry.
      p. cm. —(Smithsonian drawing books)
   Summary: "Provides information and step-by-step drawing
instructions for 30 dinosaurs"—Provided by publisher.
   ISBN 978-1-4296-8750-8 (library binding)
   ISBN 978-1-4296-9450-6 (paperback)
   1. Dinosaurs in art—Juvenile literature. 2. Drawing—
Technique—Juvenile literature. I. Title.
   NC780.5.M38 2013
   743.6—dc23   2012002682

Editorial Credits:
Kristen Mohn, editor
Alison Thiele, designer
Nathan Gassman, art director
Deirdre Barton and Eric Gohl, media researchers
Kathy McColley, production specialist

Our very special thanks to Mike Brett-Surman, PhD, Museum
Specialist for Fossil Dinosaurs, Reptiles, Amphibians, and Fish
at the National Museum of Natural History for his curatorial
review. Capstone would also like to thank Ellen Nanney
and Kealy Wilson at the Smithsonian Institution's Office of
Licensing for their help in the creation of this book.

Smithsonian Enterprises: Carol LeBlanc, Vice President;
Brigid Ferraro, Director of Licensing

Color Illustration credits:
Capstone: James Field, 3 (all), 5, 7, 11, 13, 15, 17, 23, 25,
27, 31, 35, 37, 39, 41, 43, 45, 49, 51, 53, 55, 57, 59, 61, 63,
Steve Weston, 9, 19, 21, 29, 33, 47

INTERNET SITES

FactHound offers a safe, fun way to find Internet sites
related to this book. All of the sites on FactHound have
been researched by our staff.

Here's all you do:
Visit *www.facthound.com*
Type in this code: 9781429687508
FactHound will fetch the best sites for you!

Check out projects, games and lots more at
www.capstonekids.com

Printed in the United States of America in North Mankato, Minnesota.
042012   006682CGF12